Higher Places

The Spirituality found through our dogs

ANNETTE MARIE SPIEZIO

The opinions expressed in this manuscript are solely the opinions of the author and do not represent the opinions or thoughts of the publisher. The author has represented and warranted full ownership and/or legal right to publish all the materials in this book.

Higher Places
The Spirituality found through our dogs
All Rights Reserved.
Copyright © 2015 Annette Marie Spiezio
v1.0

Cover Photo © 2015 Gina Pernini Gordon. All rights reserved - used with permission.

This book may not be reproduced, transmitted, or stored in whole or in part by any means, including graphic, electronic, or mechanical without the express written consent of the publisher except in the case of brief quotations embodied in critical articles and reviews.

Outskirts Press, Inc.
http://www.outskirtspress.com

ISBN: 978-1-4787-5997-3

Outskirts Press and the "OP" logo are trademarks belonging to Outskirts Press, Inc.

PRINTED IN THE UNITED STATES OF AMERICA

Dedication:

To Gilda and all her kin, for teaching me all I know that is good and for bringing us people to higher places.

Acknowledgement:

This book would not have taken place were it not for many people and animals, and most importantly, if not for Grace. It was written out of need and has taken its life out of love.

Thank you to Kristin Wood, who took the time out of her busy days to edit with care and much competence. Thank you to Gina Pernini-Gordon, who took the time out of her busy life, also, to create the illustrations with her care and creativity. You are both rockstars to me. Thank you to my family and friends, who encouraged and understood what this meant to me—always. Thank you to the dogs I have been privileged to know and love—my own and others. You all continue to show me the way to higher places. Above all, thank you to God for always inspiring me to the truth.

CHAPTER 1
God's Plan

Being a dog person is not something we are necessarily born with. It is a learned behavior—one prompted by simply knowing a dog. That's basically all it takes: to know, be open to, and ultimately to love a dog. I'm thinking if you are reading these pages then you have known and loved a dog—at least once. There is nothing else like it in this earthly life. I now know that our lives are changed—moved to higher places—by the honor of loving a dog. I have come to realize that I feel closest to God, to a heavenly state, when I am near my dogs—all the time, unquestionably. I believe this is an intentional plan of God's for us if we are merely open to it.

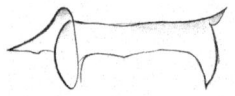

CHAPTER 2
Opening Your Heart

I was not born or even raised to be a dog person. As a matter of fact, I thought I was not one. It's like someone who says he or she is not a "winter person" when that person has never experienced the tranquil beauty of a soft winter snowfall. Or it's like someone saying he or she isn't an "exercise person" when he or she has never felt the goodness of a well-exercised body. I had never known what loving a dog would be like, so I considered myself not a dog person. I am so glad that God and the dogs had something else in mind for me. I have now come to know that, for me—and for many of you—dogs are a very important part of human development. Dogs are created by God to help us humans live in higher places. I have certainly learned much in life from many, many experiences and people, but I have not learned nearly as much from anything or anyone else than I have from my dogs.

Interestingly, none of my siblings were born "dog people" either, but all of us have been equally moved by loving so many dogs in our adult lives. Even my brother and sister-in-law, the only ones who have not had dogs, have opened their compassionate hearts to all the dogs in our families. The truth is, dogs move us all to higher places! My mom's relationship to dogs is amazing, as is she. She is actually one of those people who was bitten by a dog, two times in her childhood, and still loves all the dogs in her life. Talk about unconditional love and forgiveness—my Mom lives this.

We did have our fair share of family dogs around while I was growing up. My father owned a local restaurant and grocery store, so upon more than one occasion he would bring home a new family dog that someone had needed to find a home for. He was kind and compassionate in that way. I honestly don't even remember all the family dogs—that's how uninterested I was as a child. As I grew older there were still plenty of dogs around me. The funny thing is that many of the dogs would "take to me" much sooner than I'd "take to them." They were already trying to teach me something then.

I remember one of my sister's family dogs, named

Willy, who used to stick to me like glue when I was around. My brother-in-law and sister would laugh at how little I wanted to do with Willy, and yet he insisted that I was to be his friend. In reflection, now, I can admit that deep down Willy was transforming me, even then, to understand friendship and love and kindness. Thank you, Willy!

But oh no, I was still not a dog person. In my early adult/independent years, I would never have considered getting a dog. This had something to do with the fact that cleanliness was sort of important to me—ok, most who know me might laugh at the severity of that understatement. I was a fanatic. And, the idea of a dog bringing all of its, well, dogginess into my home was not one that appealed to me. Don't get me wrong—I like to think I was a nice enough person, so I never disliked dogs. I even wished them well and appreciated that they were God's creatures; but to me, they belonged with someone else! Someone who could "tolerate" their dogginess: dirty paws, kisses, fur etc. It was not for me!

Then my first dog came into my life: Maggie. Really into my life—I lived with her. Maggie was a mix: Wheaton terrier and spaniel. She was rescued. When I first began to share space with Maggie, I, again, tolerated her. Oh, she was kind and sweet and fun and loving, but my role with Mag was to take care of her needs—not cuddle, not bond, not love—just be responsible for her needs. And I did. I liked the role of taking care of her. I could put food down and she would eat. I could take her out and she would potty. I could tell her to sit, stay, no, etc., and she responded to me. It was kinda cool. Never having had children, I started to slightly feel the results of having this little being depend upon me and I responded with a desire to care for her. Oh, and then even on occasion, I would get impatient with Maggie and show a little dissatisfaction, and to my amazement Maggie would respond with repentance. This began to make my head tilt—kinda like dogs do when they are saying "hmmm." Maggie was kind and sensitive and she began to bring these qualities forth in me. Wow, is God ever brilliant! I began to get kind of moved by this animal, and as many would attest to, I have a "more is better" part, so low and behold, I started researching dogs—dachshunds!

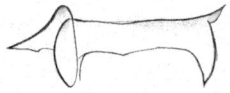

CHAPTER 3
Amazing Traits

I thought dachshunds were cool. The ones I had seen or known always seemed to have a sense of knowing something that the rest of us did not; this intrigued me. And, I actually liked their tendency toward a bit of reserve—some would call it aloofness, but I could relate to this. And, I liked that they didn't look like any other dog—one could not mistake the long torso, pointy nose, short legs, and big ears of a dachshund. I had also heard that they could be kind of funny, and I like humor. I even thought of a name for this dachshund that I was imagining in my mind: her name would be Gilda. It was a stately name, and also, I loved the late Gilda Radner, so I thought this would honor her too! The fantasy became reality before too long, and along came Gilda into my life. I could hold her in the palm of my hand—almost. She was kinda long, you know!

I should have known that this dog would have an amazing will and spirit—all dogs do! The first night we had Gilda home, we put her in a box because we hadn't gotten the proper bedding for her yet (I had no idea what "materials" were needed for a dog). I could write another book on that by now: *What Your Dog Must Have—Material Wise.* But back to the first night: we put Gilda in a box to sleep and made her very comfy with blankets, etc. The box was about eighteen inches high. We placed the box on the dining room table, tucked her in, and went to sleep. During the middle of the night, I woke to the sound of tapping on the kitchen floor. I found Gilda walking around throughout the home, exploring—all four pounds of her! The box was still standing in place, on the table. Hmmm. To this day I cannot understand how she physically got out of that box, onto the floor, and into the kitchen. Will, determination, curiosity, diligence: these are some of the amazing traits I began to learn from Gilda.

Gilda was truly my "first born." I had never imagined what kind of dedication, care and responsibility I was capable of feeling for another living being. I used to teach people, in a previous profession, that God gives us people in our lives so we can learn to be the best person we can be. We cannot do this alone, in isolation.

This is all very true, and I'm sure we can all agree that we have grown in tremendous ways by loving other human beings. What a gift that life gives us—how amazing is it to "love one another . . . as I have loved you." However, I think that many of us who have loved a dog have been given another amazing opportunity, for dogs love like no human I have ever known.

Now, please know—I am a people person to the hilt. I love people, think people are basically good, that we try our hardest and are amazing creations of God who are all on a journey together. And, I'll speak for myself, we are perfectly flawed. I am a truly rich person to have so very much human love in my life. But it seems to me that the dogs I have known are less flawed than me. And, the dogs I have known have moved me to places I would never otherwise have gone. I didn't even know love could feel this strong. With Gilda, it was not a "love at first sight" thing. I felt committed to this little being. I felt a little intrigued by her tenacity, and I felt very responsible for her, but the love came in waves—wave, after wave, after wave of Gilda moving into and ultimately taking hold of my heart. One of the first moments I remember was one sunny afternoon while I was lying on the couch resting. Gilda had, by this time, mastered the art of jumping—again, all four pounds of her, with legs the size of my thumbs. But oh no, that would not stop Gil; she could jump up on some of the furniture, but not all—yet! So up she came and she lay right upon my belly. She plopped her long nose and flappy ears on my chest and just stared into my eyes. She outstared me, and then we both fell fast asleep. Naps would never be the same for me again; I had never known how comforting it could feel to nestle up with your loyal companion. I will never forget that moment. Like they say about the Grinch: "my heart grew three times its size that day."

Gilda became like an appendage to me through the years. She, like many of the other dogs I would love, would attend to my every need. She followed me everywhere I would go and watched my every move. And I, in return, began to do the same with her. I realized as time went on that I would do very little in life without knowing and being mindful of where Gilda was, what she was doing, what she needed, and how she was. I could sense when she was uneasy about something the same way she could with me. We could "feel" each other's feelings—both emotionally and physically. And I can say with certainty that we were always right about each other. I have felt my emotion to Gil, expressed through Etta James's phenomenal song, "At Last." I sing this to Gil, even now, after she is gone, because, the emotion that is sung about in this song touches closely to what we feel with our dogs. This bond is beyond what any human bond can bring. It is faithful without negative emotion. It is loyal, it is true, it is purely unconditional, and I believe that every human is searching and yearning for this kind of connection. God knows this and tries to get us humans to relate to each other this way, but then I think God says, "Well, I know they will feel it with their dogs." This has also taught me so much about responsibility and accountability, and it was such a joy and gift to be so connected to such an amazing being. There is something quite "other worldly" about all of this. God assures us that God knows every hair on our head—every thought, feeling, and intuition we have. With Gil, I can honestly say that I was more tuned in to her than I was even to myself at times; and at other times, she told me by her attention to me what I was feeling or needing. Perhaps this kind of love is too much for us humans to extend to one another—perhaps not?

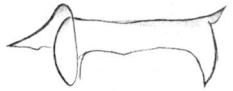

CHAPTER 4
Unconditional Love

So, Gilda and Maggie were there to teach me to love better, more like what God wants us to experience and know. I hope I was a faithful student. One day, Maggie was on a couch that Gilda could not yet get up on. She had a toy and Gilda was sitting below her on the floor, staring up in longing for the toy. She didn't cry or bark; she just stared. Maggie nosed the toy down to the floor for Gilda to enjoy. Wow—I thought that Mag was sweet before, but she had just risen to sainthood in my book. Maggie constantly showed me how to give without expecting anything in return. This is the way God wants us all to love: unconditionally and without any expectation in return. Maggie was my first canine instructor in this. Any treat, any affection, anything you gave to Maggie—she appreciated with so much gratitude and no assumption whatsoever. What would our world be like if more of us humans loved like Maggie? It would be a place where love was a free gift, given and received freely. I think that is what God had in mind. That is why God sent the Maggies!

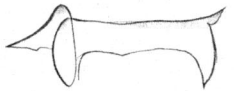

CHAPTER 5
More Amazing Traits

Gilda was all about learning—another higher virtue. She was a student of life and dedicated to success upon every step she took. Oh, not in a competitive manner. Gilda was all about doing what was right: what was expected, what was needed. She was a worker, an explorer, and a succeeder. Then, she would turn around and do something silly to make us laugh—she knew the value of hard work and hard play! She was great at both. Gilda delighted in others' laughter and would repeat behavior that prompted laughter from us. But, she also would win medals in agility at training school and mix it up with all the big dogs in her class. She and everyone else around her knew: her spirit and will and strength were far larger than her physical size. So, again, she knew the beauty of hard work and hard play. She had fervor beyond belief.

Another example of Gilda's understanding of hard work and hard play was a parade! One year, her dog class was to march in a local Fourth of July parade. Gil was about two years old; she was the smallest in her class and the parade was pretty long, but we all thought she could do it. It was a warm July day and tons of fun. Gil LOVED getting dressed up—but ever so classily. She was not one for froufrou outfits or silly costumes, so that day I believe we just spruced her up in a new collar and perhaps a cool T-shirt. Then, off she went—we went—marching in this parade with a pack of big dogs. She marched right in step, following the music and drums and delighting in all the fun that was happening around her, and, she never missed a beat, But it was a long parade; she, and all the dogs, were so very tired and thirsty at the end. It was lovely to me, how people along the way—spectators—wanted to offer the dogs water and ice. Gilda would step up to receive a refreshing drink and then lick the person to say thank you. She had impeccable manners, and stamina beyond belief! That day was a most memorable and delightful day for Gil and I; I couldn't have been more proud of her.

CHAPTER 6
Journeys

So, on went our journey together. Gilda adapted to many changes in her life: some health issues early on; moving a few times; losing Maggie in her life; then incorporating a new sister, Molly, who was another dachshund. Molly was more of the gentle-spirit type, like Maggie had been. Molly was a rescue dog and I got her when she was about five years old; Gil was about three then. Gilda knew deep down that it was time to welcome Molly into her world, and she did so tenderly, playfully, and lovingly. She must have understood early on that Molly had had a very rough life up to now, and it was up to us to change Mol's life for the better. So, that is what we did. Molly also changed ours—of course. She was sweet and humble and so appreciative of everything and anything we gave her—which of course made me want to give her everything in the world. See how this kind of love works? When we give and receive with no expectation we want to give more and more. God knew this! That is why God sent the Mollys into the world—to show us this kind of assumptionless love.

It was interesting that Molly was a bit fearful—and remained so her entire life—of certain things: loud voices, fast movements, etc. This indicated to me the sad truth that she may have been abused. However, she amazingly became trusting of Gilda and I very early on, and, also of the people who we lovingly brought into her life. Again—her instincts were keen, and like so many amazing dogs, when you tell them they are safe and loved they believe you 'til the end. This is another quality that would be so useful for us humans to develop better: the art of believing! Without reserve, if someone says he or she loves us and will stay with us forever, believe it, enjoy it, and love it! If God says we are children who are loved, believe it. How much time do we spend doubting—even doubting God's love at times? And if we loved and believed like Molly, we might be having a more peaceful existence. Molly did! She really enjoyed her life. She, Gilda, and I had a pretty fun thing going. They became true sisters—sharing, protecting each other, playing, exploring together, and truly loving each other. It was interesting as well that Gilda knew pretty early on that Molly was to be the alpha between them. She knew to respect her elder—even though she also knew that her own skills and leadership were probably stronger in some ways. But it was Molly's place, at the time, to be leader. Gilda showed great humility then and for many years to come.

We eventually moved into another home where Gil and Mol had a fair amount of "run of the home"—a fenced-in yard, gardens, walkways, a living room couch in front of a window to do their guarding of the house, and so on and so on! They loved our yard. They were great gardeners—in fact, they taught me a true love of gardening. All of our favorite activity was when we could be outside together: put on some John Denver or Crosby, Stills, and Nash music, get the gardening gear on, and have at it! We loved it. Gil especially would diligently follow me around every step. She would explore my new plantings and check out the progress of the old. She enjoyed smelling the dirt and didn't mind getting a little dirty herself. However, whether I taught this to her or not (probably so!), she also wanted to be cleaned up and enjoyed doing so before she entered the home. She was a hard worker; she would stay out there with me for hours, long after Molly would have said, "Enough—I'm going in to the cool home!" Gil was there—every hour, every garden. She truly gave me the gift of love of gardening.

Oh, and Mol, on the other hand, helped her share too. Mostly she was interested in what parts of the garden she could eat; she did enjoy her food. So, we would find her in the veggie garden, snacking on tomatoes (I know—dogs aren't supposed to have tomatoes, but Molly seemed to do fine with them), or sniffing out the peppers (didn't care for them), or Molly sometimes enjoyed just a good hunk of dirt! Again—so much appreciation to be learned from them. I owe my passion for gardening to Mol and Gil! They also both enjoyed just a good, long sunbeam to lie in—inside or outside our home. This always reminded me of John Denver's song, "Sunshine," which I love and which my dogs always seemed to really get into as well. "Sunshine, almost always, makes me high!" Again, I never stopped to appreciate the warmth and beauty of an awesome sunbeam until I witnessed the soothing stillness that it brought to Molly and Gilda.

Gilda was so full of life, and I believe she literally brought Molly back to life and youthfulness again within about a year of them being together. Molly was definitely physically less fit and certainly not as agile as Gilda, but once Gilda's spirit would infuse a situation, Molly started to realize how fun it was and how life could actually be fun and loving, all at once! One of Gil's favorite games was to do "down-dog" to Molly and then DASH—I mean tear-ass—around the yard to get her to chase her. Gilda was lightning fast in her day, and they were both pretty low to the ground, so you can visualize how amazing they looked when tearing around the yard. Molly was wise about it, knowing her physical limitations. She would fake and wait! Gil knew what she was doing and also adapted to Molly's physical limitations—she kept playing the game, making Molly feel good about it and both having fun together. Again—amazing is an understatement to describe how instinctually sensitive and adaptive they both were to giving enjoyment to the other!

Watching a dog interact with life can teach us so very much about life, and specifically about how God wants us to live and appreciate life. Taking walks is a good example of this. Prior to having dogs, I would never think of taking a walk as a fun or stimulating exercise. Today, I look forward to our walks—every single day—as one of the best parts of my day. Rain or shine, it is truly one of my favorite times of the day. This was taught to me, especially, by Gilda. Gilda thought of her walks as a responsibility, but one that she fully embraced and looked forward to every day. She, like so many of the other dogs I have had, would start to turn happy circles and get very animated and excited when she knew it was time. Sometimes I would tell her a bit early about our plans—so she could enjoy the anticipation; we all enjoy a little anticipation. She learned early on, and was committed to being a part of the neighborhood—getting out there, mixing it up, saying hello to friendly people, checking out what has been happening, making sure everything was in order, safe, and right. This was Gilda's job, and what better place to exercise that than on a walk. She, like me, enjoyed all the elements.—well, neither of us held cold rain as a favorite, but, hey, we muddled through. Gil taught me this, too; get through it if it's the right thing to do.

What was most enlightening about walking my dogs though, through these past fifteen years or so, is their sheer curiosity, appreciation, and delight in everything God has made. I could get lost for hours watching them sniff the grass, the trees—Gilda was especially fond of pines—the flowers. They were sometimes frightened by yard statues. (I am sometimes frightened by yard statues myself!) They appreciated the sun, they walked more intently when the weather was a little inclement, and Gilda was always the leader on walks, whichever dog/s she was with. She got it. She dug it. She led it. Once in a while, I would have to remind Gil that I was in charge and we weren't making this or that turn. By the way, Gilda also learned her directions; if I said "go left, Gil," she would turn left—it was quite amazing. Her strong will would rise up on occasion, but once she understood that I meant business, she, again, did the right thing, with no begrudging at all. I do owe my appreciation of God's amazing work in nature to my dogs—all of them.

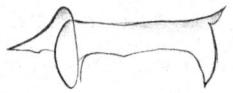

CHAPTER 7
Moderation

Many dogs I have known have also taught me much about the wind—and moderation. My mom also taught me much about the virtue of living with moderation. I am indebted to both. With the wind, Gilda, Molly, and Karly, who you will later hear about, loved the wind—in moderation. They would show sheer delight and wonder at a cool summer or spring breeze. They loved the feel of running through it; they loved having their ears fly back—or in Karly's case, her fur. They even enjoyed the gentle sound of a nice humming wind. Oh, and Gilda loved to put her head out the window during car rides; I think she also got a bit of a kick out of watching other people in cars laugh at her big flappy ears in the wind; she was a bit of a clown, you know! But, when it came to too strong of winds, none of them liked it. They did not enjoy loud noises or heavy wind against them. They liked moderation, a little being just enough. Oh, how I and others could learn from this. They knew about "enough" and were totally satisfied with a moderate life rather than one of excess.

Gilda also understood the laws of nature, but with the kind and good spirit that she had. One time, while on a walk (I must not have been paying attention to her; I believe I was stopped to pick up some of Molly's "business"), I turned around and Gilda had a squirrel in her mouth; the squirrel was alive and struggling. Gil had not "attacked" it, she had just "gotten it." I yelled very sternly at her to drop it—a command she knew. Right in front of my eyes she dropped the squirrel and looked up at me with those huge eyes, as if to say, "Sorry, I didn't mean to do anything wrong; it was just my instinct." I was moved by her kindness—of letting go of something so instinctual to her just to obey me and do the right thing. Again—godly characteristics—I think so. She was able to control her instincts to a higher good. Isn't this what God wants for all of our earthly lives, to strive every day to a higher purpose, a heavenly one?

Molly also loved a good encounter with a squirrel and she taught me something many dogs teach—patience and perseverance. Molly would run faster than ever when she spotted or sensed a squirrel up in one of our trees. (Well, she ran kind of fast for treats as well!) When she found a squirrel, though, she would position herself underneath that tree and stare—just stare—fixated on the squirrel's every move. Molly would not, could not be distracted—actually, not even with the promise of a treat. Oh no, this was important business and it was not to be interrupted. Her job was to make that squirrel leave our yard, and nothing would stop her until she accomplished her task. I used to worry that she was going to get a stiff neck, because she would stare up for what seemed like an hour.—perhaps it was a little less. And then there would be some barking—oh yes, of course, because when the squirrel did not exit by her stare she needed to assert herself more to let the squirrel know exactly whose yard this was. This was Molly's most important task in life, but as in everything, Molly taught me so much more than protecting the yard from squirrels. She showed me the power of patience and perseverance, the power to stay with it and never give up. This was a great lesson to witness over and over again with sweet Mol.

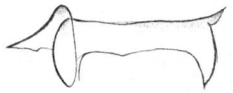

CHAPTER 8
Patience/Music

Speaking of patience, I learned a tremendous amount about patience from my dogs, when I consider how they moved through their days—with steadiness, consistency, and patience, always, every day. They need and love consistency. They do not think of repetition as boredom, as we do. In fact—they teach us great things about boredom. They seem to find the extraordinary in the ordinary of everyday living. For the most part, they do the same thing, every day, and, they don't complain—in fact, they thrive on it. They look forward to their meals, their rest time, their walks, their work, their play, their cuddle time—day in and day out, just the same. Most of us can attest, that our dogs do get a little "thrown" when their routines are changed, but, again, like true, brave champs they adjust and form a new routine. What they really need is consistency and dependability! Meals are a great example of this. Basically, they eat the same food at the same time every day. And, every day, they look forward to it, are grateful for it, are sustained by it, and enjoy it: same food, same treats, same plan. They don't get bored. They don't need "diversions" like we do. They are also patient with time. They live the saying, "live life, on life's terms." Wow, what we can learn from this! They wait for us humans to be ready for what they need. Walks, cuddle, play, food—they wait, patiently, without complaint. Oh, how I can learn from this. They are content with the ordinary. They are also patient with how they feel. They don't run from a little pain or discomfort—they wait through it. They do not look for constant escapes, diversions, or numbing from real life. They are brave and patient. Again, at least this human has so very much to learn. I try to model and learn from them, about staying in the moment and living life on life's terms.

Gilda and Molly also helped me with my meditation practice. It's amazing how well dogs learn and adapt to the flow of life, of a day. They are ready to play, eat, rest, relax, play, eat—again and again—without any need for diversions. They seem to understand the natural and healthy flow of life—if we allow it to happen. When I was practicing a regular meditation daily, Gil and Mol used to know it was time for this and take their positions near me. They would literally understand that I was going to meditate at that time, and their role was to do this with me. So, there we would sit—the three of us—in a quite, meditative position, with either meditation tapes or silence for up to a half hour. Often, having Gil and Mol present with me was a strong vehicle for me to a state of holiness. Sometimes, just touching them, or watching their steady breathing, would bring me closer to God.

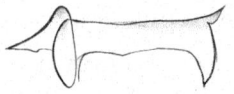

CHAPTER 9
Language

I often wish that my dogs could talk—I mean really talk the language I speak. However, I've come to understand their language and really appreciate it. I've thought on more than one occasion that I use too many words anyway. I was fortunate enough to travel to Italy a few times, several years ago, and though my family and I tried to learn a bit more Italian before we went, suffice it to say we had to communicate there with less-than-proficient language. But we loved it! Part of the magic of those trips was using gestures, affection, kindness, and instincts to communicate with our Italian relatives and people we'd encounter along the way. It was amazing, and quite cool, that our gestures, eye contact, physical touch, and sounds could express more than a thousand words. Dogs do this. They communicate everything they need without words. They give us love, affection, respect and the like—all without words. It's almost as if they know something we don't because they exist and relate to life without words. Though I must add—Gil kinda did talk. Of course, I believe she was truly exceptional, but sometimes I feel she came so close to using her own language through sounds and expression. And, I believe that dogs do understand many, many things we say—more than some people think they do. Gilda and some of my other dogs came to fully understand a number of phrases. "Wanna go for a ride in the car?" would prompt utter excitement—dashing through the home, running toward the door and leashes. "Turn left/turn right/go across/look both ways"—Gilda knew all these phrases, and to my amazement, every time, she obeyed the command. "I'm gonna get the collar . . . or squirt gun"—Gilda and then Karly and Eli knew that this meant they were doing something that they needed to stop—likely barking—and by merely saying the phrase, they would cease. Amazing! I also wished my dogs could smile when they were happy. Some people say their dogs do; mine never really had a smile. Oh, of course, I understand the meaning of a wagging tail or a drop to their back for a tummy rub clear as a bell. But, I've come to appreciate and learn from the fact that dogs don't smile. I think they understand the sometimes seriousness of life. Not to get all dark on you here, but I think life is challenging. I try to see the love and beauty, and no, I don't wear black all the time. I like a good party and bright things and fun—but I do see life as pretty serious. Perhaps this has something to do with my profession—so be it. But I have learned from my dogs that it is ok to see the seriousness of life and then turn around and roll, wrestle, play, and enjoy the moments that God gives us for joy. So, I totally relate to the fact that our dogs don't smile—they know!!

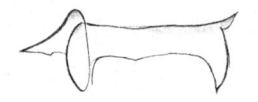

CHAPTER 10
More Journeys

Many people, events, and places came and went in our lives. Gilda and Molly won the hearts of many—as do most dogs I know. They were fortunate to be loved by many and lived in the "it takes a village" mentality. For a spell, my niece Gina lived with us. This was an amazing year-plus for us all and Gil and Mol simply loved Gina and her spirit and presence in our lives, as did I! And then it was time to move homes again.

We moved into a new home gradually. In this home lived a 150-pound Newfoundland named Kona. Kona was the ultimate gentle giant, as Newfoundlands are so lovingly referred to. She was kind and gentle and unassuming and patient. She welcomed Gilda and Molly into her world with all these qualities and more. Gilda and Molly were very lucky to have Kona be so welcoming and sweet to them. Because of their size difference and because of the place we moved into being Kona's home, the three of them never really established a pack-like relationship. Kona was a little old and not in good enough physical shape to take walks, so the rhythms of the three were not in sync. But, aside from that, they, again, all adapted and got along like champs—something not all humans are capable of doing. Oh, we try, but sometimes our humanness gets in the way and we get more territorial. But not these three—Kona, Gil and Mol all learned to live happily in this new configuration. Only five months after we moved in we all had to say good-bye to Kona. She was struggling with health issues and it was time to let her go. There was a grieving in the home, of course, that Gilda and Molly didn't necessarily feel that strongly because they never bonded that much with Kona, but they were sensitive to the loss that everyone else felt—a deep loss for lovely, beautiful, and loving Ms. Kona. Not long after this brief transitional stage, we all packed up and moved to our more permanent home, where we have stayed. This new home had a pool, gardens galore to build, many new rooms and space to explore, wonderful family and friends around us, and a great neighborhood, so low and behold, Gilda and Molly once again had the run of the home to some degree! They were back to their couch in the window to guard the neighborhood, back to gardening with me in the summers, back to fabulous walks around our neighborhood, back to a very fun and loving home with lots to do and love of family and friends constantly surrounding them.

I learned much through all this about being adaptive and welcoming to change in my life. Most human beings, including this one, take some adjustment, of course, to changes. Whether it's moving homes, health issues, changes in relationships, jobs, etc.—our worlds need some routine to feel stable. Dogs need this, too, but they have more faith. It's just like the virtue of trusting and believing that I mentioned earlier. They adjust to newness very quickly because they trust and know that you must pick up your bootstraps, build in new routines, and move forward. God definitely gave me these animals to set examples of how to adjust. Gilda had epilepsy from two years old on. She had a minor disc problem in her back from about six years old on. She moved seven times in twelve years, but stayed luckily in two great homes for five years and in her last for three years, so some of the moves were quick. But through all this, she never complained, never lost her fervor, her drive, her discipline, her goodness, her joy and wonder—she stayed in the moment as much as she could and truly lived in a higher place. Gilda had great strength, almost every day of her life. She taught me so very much about this. I have been pretty fortunate with a healthy body thus far in my life, except for a migraine condition. I think it is no accident that God sent me Gilda with her epilepsy to show me how to endure. And she did. She got through adjustments to medicines, recovered from seizure,s and kept her positive spirit through it all. I oftentimes, and still today for sure, call upon Gilda's strength to help me get through things when I'm not feeling well. I try to be more like her and persevere even I feel like giving up. I will never give up—thanks to Gilda, thanks to God! So, Gilda and Molly really enjoyed our new home/family/yard/neighborhood, etc. We had a great first year—then Molly's health began to decline.

Molly taught us all much about strength and stamina. She had a rough start to life, then had what I hope were about eight very happy and loving years with us and the life around us. She showed me how to put the past behind and be appreciative of the moment. She was a most appreciative being for everything: love, food, affection (though she took some time to get comfortable with affection), a warm bed. I remember when I first got Molly and was told she had always slept in her crate—again, she was probably about five years old at that point. The very first night—while I was living with Gilda alone at that point—Gilda and I decided that Molly definitely needed to see what sleeping in a bed with us was like. You would have thought I gave Molly the world on a string! She curled up into that bed with Gil and I and looked up at me with two of the most grateful, loving, genuine brown eyes I had ever known. From that moment on, Molly was always the first in bed at night!

Molly especially taught me a true appreciation for napping! Now mind you, I already was a pretty good napper all my life. I like the rhythm of hard work and good rest on repeat! Like Gilda, I understand this. But until you feel the utter joy in lying next to your canine companions for a snuggle every day, you can never imagine how good a nap can be. And to see and feel their pure joy in being able to rest with you—there is nothing like it. If they could talk, I think they'd say, "Job well done to us all—let's reward ourselves with some rest, comfort, closeness, and rejuvenation!" There is nothing in the world like napping with our loving dogs. And they themselves have not only been there for me to do this, but they have showed me just how much to appreciate this precious time.

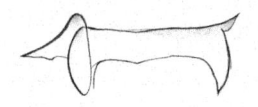

CHAPTER 11
Love and Loss

After a year now in our new home, Molly's body began to fail her. Up to the end, she remained faithful, loving, patient, grateful, and kind. Nancy built her a ramp to help her get around; we made more beds for her, and Gilda took very good care of her spirit, trying to slip in a quick game of "bite me" once in a while, which, even in Mol's pain, she again tried to please Gil by participating. Molly wanted us all to know—including Gilda—that we had saved her life and she was so thankful to have had a happy life for the majority of her time on earth. I couldn't thank Molly enough for trusting me, for letting me know and love her grateful, gentle, mellow spirit. Molly gave very few kisses out in her life, but on rare occasion, if I asked her, she would give me one kiss at a time. This was such a gift. I told

Molly every day of her life with me that she was staying with me forever and she knew this was true. She taught me so much about being in the moment and not carrying past burdens around. That is something I think God wants for us all—to start each day with appreciation and openness. Molly did this, most especially when her day started surrounded by the people/beings she loved—and breakfast! And God, and God's nature around her: she knew it all was sooo good. She wasn't quite the worker that Gilda was, but she appreciated Gilda's strong work ethic; once in a while, she'd join her sister in a task that needed to be done, like barking at the mail carrier, other dogs, squirrels, playing chase, moving pine cones around, etc. Mol would step up to the task if she saw Gil needed a little companionship or simply reinforcement. Interesting, again, that Molly—though she was theoretically Alpha with Gil—was not a micromanager. She would be happy to sit back and let Gilda do her jobs, with the confidence that Gilda would do her jobs well. Wouldn't it be nice, if whenever possible, we humans could trust people to do their jobs without micromanaging? We could empower one another, like Gilda and Molly did each other.

Molly got to say good-bye to so many people in her life who loved her before we said our good-bye. We are extremely fortunate to have had amazing nieces, friends, neighbor friends, and more family all to love our dogs with us. Every dog I have had the privilege of loving has also had the privilege of being loved by all of these amazing people in my life. Again, it takes a village! Wow, how truly blessed we all are.

After we said good-bye to Molly, it was again a very sad time in our home. Gilda spent about two days ripping the shreds out of some of her toys; we let her. She was in pain, as were we all. I didn't quite know how to help Gilda through this grief, except to share in it with her. We would hold each other and talk about how bad it felt. I learned early on that talking to our dogs about what was really going on was helpful. For example, I told Molly every single day of her life with me that she was staying with us forever. I believe that after some time Molly understood and felt what this meant. So, I continued to talk to my dogs. Sometimes it is easier to explain things to them than it is to the people in my life, perhaps because they listen. They try so hard to "take in" and understand what I am saying. As a counselor by profession, I work every day with people in and out of relationships to become more understanding and compassionate to one another. This is all God would ask of us—to understand and be compassionate. And I firmly believe that if we all held higher levels of compassion and understanding for one another then we would live in a much more loving place—within and without our lives. So, once again, our dogs have taught us this throughout time. They listen, they try to understand, and wow, do they have compassion! Sometimes, when I was having a big feeling—positive or negative—Gilda or Molly would come up to me and simply begin to lick my face or nudge their head into my lap, or put a paw on my hand. I always felt and interpreted this as validation—pure validation. They were saying to me, "I know you're feeling sad, worried, happy, curious, and I understand." Wow—if we could only just do this with one another. So, when Molly died, we all spent a lot of time simply validating each other.

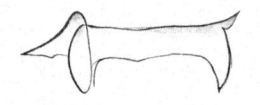

CHAPTER 12
Love and Gain

It only took about a week for us to realize that Gilda was not meant to be alone, nor were we meant to be a one-dog family.

It is funny how dogs, guided by God's energetic plan, choose us—we don't chose them! I had a friend once who said that about pumpkins! Perhaps so, but dogs for sure choose us. The way in which this happens with animals, dogs especially, has showed me that we must be awake and pay attention to what God, through life, is trying to show us. It's this instinctual nature of life that we need to be open and awake to, like our dogs show us to be. There is so much that we miss because we are asleep to life around us. Not dogs—they are alert when awake, relaxed when relaxing, and asleep when sleeping! Imagine this!

So, the events that led to the arrival of our new dog, Karly, were quite amazing—but not a surprise, because, again dogs live in these higher places all the time. We are completely convinced that Molly also had a hand in assisting God in bringing us Karly. What is also amazing is that Karly exemplified many of Molly's characteristics and mannerisms when she got here. We were constantly amazed and wonderfully comforted by all of this: he connection, the circle of life, ahhhhhhh, if we just pay attention.

My niece had had a dog named Tuffy who I really dug. I didn't know him that well, but the few times I met and interacted with Tuffy I thought, what a nice guy! He is! Just super friendly, playful, loving—I liked this guy. During that week with Gil alone, during our grief, we started thinking about what to do next. I texted my niece, "Hey, Deanne, what breed is Tuffy?" "Havanese," she replied. Hmmm, I had never known much about Havanese. At the same time, Nancy was calling her friends at our local pet store to just inquire about what new breeds/litters they had in. When we compared notes, we were not shocked to find out that we both had learned about Havanese and low and behold the pet store had just gotten a new litter in and they had some baby girls still there. Within twenty-four hours we brought Karly home to our family.

Gilda—still in her grief only one week after Molly had left us—was not certain at first how she felt about Karly. Oh, she did not want to hurt her—Gilda would never hurt anything in life—but she was not quite ready to open her heart and home to her instantly. She was intrigued, and I'm sure she thought she was as cute as could be, but she stayed close to me and did much checking her out. Occasionally, she would let out this low, humming kind of noise, as if to say, "Ohhhhh, I think you're pretty cool, but I don't know what's happening here." Now mind you—Karly is an angel. When we went to the pet store to meet her—first Nancy and then I—she took to us immediately. She ran around this little pen and rolled over, playing "show off," if you will, to the point that one of Nancy's daughters, who was with us, said to her mom, "So, Mom, what's the question?"! Indeed, there was none. Karly picked us. And, Karly—who we lovingly refer to as our little "Hippie"—is as kind and joyful and loving and peaceful a spirit as you will ever come across. Gilda definitely knew this from the onset as well. But, she was going through her own emotional adjustment. So, one morning, as Gilda was sitting on my lap and Karly was kind of scampering around her, I was nervously holding Gilda back. Nancy said, "Let her go." She told Gilda, "Go ahead, Gil, go get her if you want." So, I let her go and Gilda and Karly began their bond. It was sweet and loving and kind on both of their parts—all at once. Within days they began to play and cuddle and share their family together. Dogs are truly amazing; they know how to welcome and love as God would have us to do. And Gilda was now being kept young by this new sister in her life, Karly. Again, the circles continue.

Karly truly came to us to bring Gilda, and us all, back to life. And, she was very happy to have been chosen by us. She loved Gilda; she kind of idolized her and was ever so willing to have her as her leader. And Gilda, well, as you might suspect, loved having this new job and responsibility in life. Karly had her fair share of puppy mischief, for which Gilda would discipline her. It was great—she was basically raising Karly to be a good dachshund! But Karly also held her own—as a true Havanese. She would not be as committed to work and walks—she was much more prone toward kisses and cuddling and enjoying the breeze. She is a hippie! She likes to peace-out.

She and Gilda's spirits would meet on certain things, like the park. Gilda thought of the park as another place to manage. She liked the open pasture of it; she enjoyed when there were children playing—as there "should" be, in Gil's world. She liked that we would run through it. Karly, on the other hand, just simply loved that it was such a happy place. When we would get even remotely close to the park, Karly would start circling Gil and razzing her up and getting very excited. When at the park, Karl would start to down-dog and dash and try to get Gil going into a good game of wrestle and play. It was such a joy to see their sheer delight in the park. I will never take for granted again the joy of a park. Couldn't we all use a little more park in our lives?!

Karly is also a great stretcher—something we can also learn from. Oh, most dogs are pretty good and awfully cute when they stretch, but Karls—well, this is a spiritual thing for her. She loves to move her body in the morning to get the energy flowing; you can almost see her wake up to herself, the day, and God's universe with her stretching. It is very prolonged and very soothing all at once. She would really dig yoga—in fact, she may have invented it somewhere along the line. She understands good energy: how to hold it, how to spread it, how to create it around her. When Karly is around, people smile. She brings on happiness because she is committed to happiness. And peace, she likes her peace. She is kinda like a little Ghandi—wise and humble and a true mediator in life. More on this later, re Karls.

So Gil and Karly spent one year together learning to be perfect sisters. They never fought, they loved to play, they shared well, they watched out for each other, and yet they allowed each other to be an individual. I love to learn how to get along from our dogs—wow, do they know something about adaptation, acceptance and love. They understand also that we were not meant to be alone. Gilda had always been a part of a pack—small packs, but packs nonetheless. She liked belonging, and, she was quite willing to be in charge, for the rest of her life, once Molly was gone. It's like she grew up but thankfully still kept her youthful playfulness. And, she definitely kept her sense of humor—something we all need to keep. One day, while we were gathered out in our yard, Gilda entertained the group in a memorable way. There were several friends spread out across the pool on the lounge chairs just relaxing, listening to the sounds of summer and music; Gil and Karl were mingling about. We were getting ready to barbecue some hot dogs for lunch. The hot dogs were waiting on a table near grill. Gilda could always jump higher than any being with that short of legs should be able to, so, you might fill in the story. While we weren't watching—because Gil would never do this while we were watching—she jumped up on the chair, then onto the table, and grabbed a hot dog in her mouth. There she stood, posed, on the table, this amazing wiener dog, with a big ole hot dog dangling out of both sides of her mouth. There was an outburst of laughter like no other. Gilda loved this—she had just put on the perfect show for all her friends. Oh, but once we got ahold of ourselves and ran to get the dog out of her mouth she consumed it, of course. She was no dummy. Karly sat and watched, spinning around in circles, joyful that so much fun was happening. She was always happy to have Gil be the "wind beneath her wings," for sure.

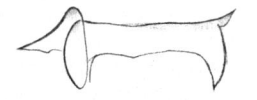

CHAPTER 13
Express Yourself

Karly knows something about expressing herself and "letting it out." From when she was a pup, and we were still trying to get her to sleep in her crate, very early on, she let us know that there would be no sleeping in the crate. I've come to understand that this was not because she was being naughty; Karly is just an incredibly social creature. She loves people. She knows much about friendship. She lives for it! She so appreciates the gift of a loving friend, and when she is feeling a void of any kind, such as her relationships, she howls. It comes from deep within her. It sometimes starts in a high-pitched cry, very pathetic, and then works its way to a full-out howl: nose up in the air, perched-up howl. She is great at it, and she is not afraid to show her feelings. Karly has come to be very fond of her little friend next door, Daisy. Daisy looks just like Karl, so when they do get a play date, it's hard to tell who is who once they start running and razzing around. If Karly is in our yard, though, and Daisy goes out into hers, it's howling time. Or, if Daisy walks by the front walk: howling time. On a sadder note, when Gilda left us, after a couple days, when Karl realized she was really gone, she howled randomly for days. So, Karly has taught me much about expressing my feelings. And, sometimes, don't we all just need a good howl?

Another way Karly has taught me much about being free to express myself is by her spinning! Yes, Karly loves to spin. When we first started observing Karly and her spinning, we thought it meant only one thing—nervousness or uncertainty. And in fact, sometimes when Karls is nervous or uncertain, she will spin. However, as time goes on, we have come to recognize that the "spin" means several different things. Her circles can mean joy, they can mean excitement, they can mean thoughtfulness—kind of like the human version of pacing. Which, by the way, Gilda actually did pace when she was pondering a situation—back and forth—while Karly does circles. She, Karly, is such an instinctual being—she lets it out, she does not hide her internal world. She spins, she howls, she rolls on her back—she's all over it, all of it. I think Karls lives life so in the moment, and for this, I am so grateful for what she is teaching me about trying to do the same.

Yes, Karly has taught me much about being present and open to feelings and the love that lies within her. Taking our walks is a good example of this. Every living being I know is driven into action by some motivation, whether it be instinctual or thought out. This is not a bad thing; it is more of a cause and effect characteristic about being alive. And, it is good to understand and be aware of our drives and desires. This is a holy thing and God wants us to be true to our natural desires. Dogs do this so very well. As for walks, it has been very clear to me what motivated and still motivates each of my dogs. Maggie wanted to please us; Molly wanted to be a part of the pack and also to receive a treat reward. Eleanor, who you will learn about later, wants to do something—she likes to keep busy. Life is her playground. Gilda, you might have guessed, wanted to do her job. She needed—and I mean needed—to get out everyday, into the neighborhood, and make sure things were in order as they should be. She needed to let the neighborhood know that she was doing her part to be in charge and that she would keep things in order. Oh, and that there were not to be too many yard statues—as previously mentioned, she did not care for them. So, yes, she had a job, and she felt accomplished and faithful to perform this job every single day—through rain or shine. Gilda also took quite seriously the job of teaching and leading Karly and then Eleanor on our walks. She was patient with their puppiness, but she stayed steady in her leadership. You could tell she was so excited to incorporate Karly and then Eleanor into the pack for walks. It's as if she was showing off her two baby sisters when we walked—all four of us—and how well they were learning to follow her. Now, Karly has one desire on her walks: to meet up with people or dogs. More people, then dogs, and even more specifically, she would love to play with every child who is riding a bike, kicking a ball, swinging on a swing, or jumping rope. When walking, Karly gets adamant about going in the direction of the action. Her tail wags—really her whole butt wags as she see's something fun happening. But she's not just about the fun; she is very excited about the people. It's as if she is saying, "Oh, look, how fun are people, children, dogs—let's get together." She may have inspired Bob Marley, "Let's get together and feel all right." That's our Karls. What I have learned from her utter gratitude and love for others is to try to have some of the same. Oh, I do know every day of my life how incredibly blessed I am to have so many gifts of life in my life: family, friends, neighbors, my work, and of course, my dogs. But what I don't do as well as Karly is express this, or stay present to each opportunity to be with those I love. Perhaps this is called a bit of taking it all for granted, perhaps it is a part of me that gets tired sometimes, but in witnessing Karly's joy for others it has helped me to be more joyful for the simple gift of love that surrounds my life.

This also goes along with something else Karly teaches us every day: being nice matters. We have a sign in our kitchen that reads, "Because Nice Matters," and I believe this. I do try to live it because kindness and niceness mean the world to me. I believe they mean the world to all of us. Karly gets this. She does not have room in her world for anything but niceness and kindness. She shows this even in the gentle way she moves about. She is soft and light on her feet. She does not impose herself upon you; she will always sit next to you and wait to be invited to come on your lap. The same is true in the bed; she will be invited to come up on the bed and will wait at the foot of the bed to be invited to come closer. And, if she doesn't get invited, she does not complain; she stays at the foot, contently. Yes, Karly knows the virtue of kindness and patience. Another example of her patience is with her food. She waits nicely when her meal is being made. She trusts that it will come, in time, and she does not need to hurry you. She believes in you, and if you said you are getting her meal, she knows it will come. She also likes to do things slowly and in her time. If she is given a treat, she prefers to take it to her designated spot and sits it down and waits there 'til she is ready. This could be for minutes and often much longer, but nothing rushes Karly. She prefers slow, methodical movement and procedures in life. She does not like abruptness. She likes to move with a bit of a groove, and this includes niceness and patience. Karly does not expect anything in return for her kindness; she just likes it!

I think most dogs I have known have great manners! This is amazing to me, because we claim that their brain capacity is so different from humans, yet they get things far better than at least this human, for sure! To me, they are always polite. Sure, they can show great excitement for moments; they can sometimes bark as a result of their doing their jobs, and yes, they can make some bodily messes. But, the dogs I have known almost seem apologetic when they make a mess. Or, humbly ready to back off if their emotions get too high. They recognize that manners matter. Gilda also had excellent manners with people. She would most often greet all people in a respectful way. She knew what was right and wrong. You say hi to people, you act kind, and then you can take your space if you need it. She was polite and correct. Karly and Eli, being pretty young, tried to learn a lot from Gilda in terms of these social norms or manners, but they still have to learn the art of trust, since Gilda is gone. Again, all dogs seem to know that respect and patience and manners are real important in life. They help everyone to feel better about things. I hope I can embody this as well.

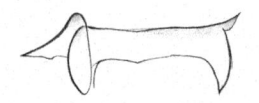

CHAPTER 14
And Now We Work

Gilda always showed her love for you through acts of work, responsibility, and taking care of things. You knew that she was doing her work out of love for you. In fact, when I'd come home, she would of course come to greet me, but she would immediately run to her toy, whatever she was doing, as if to say, "See, Mom, I've been busy doing this or that." This was so Gil. She showed affection by acts of work. There is actually a book written about this called the "Five Languages of Love" that talks about how we all have our preferred ways of giving and receiving love. For Karly, hers is presence; for Gilda, hers was work. Gilda had many jobs around our homes. I have mentioned her many jobs outside in the gardens and neighborhood. She also was dutiful about barking away anything or anyone she deemed "not welcome," which included, but was not limited to: mail carriers, deliveries, work people, landscapers, wind, thunder, lightning, fireworks, and the list goes on and on. But we all knew Gil really meant well. She believed that if and when she barked these things would go away, so it was her job to do so. Gilda also had another job that amazed us and our people when we would be sitting around the deck and pool. This was pinecone removal. We have many pinecones from surrounding trees along the deck. Gilda felt she must be working; I think she kinda felt it was her job to earn her stay. I have always felt this way in life, too—perhaps one of us gave that instinct to the other? In any case, for Gil, she had to be working or else she would take a rest. Again, I can relate to this. But she would start shortly after people arrived, and she would give them the appropriate greeting, then she would march pinecones across the deck. She would gather them from one side then march them across to the other, then sometimes chew on them, or at other times just leave them there for her sisters to play with. If she was in a more nervous mood, she would stop occasionally and chew them on the deck. She meant no harm; she just needed to stay busy. We all respected and appreciated her hard work ethic. I know many people—including myself—who have this kind of need to work, to be busy. So, I hope everyone knows that like Gil, we totally enjoy your company and having people in our lives; we just sometimes feel we have to earn our keep.

Another job of Gilda's was to patrol the area each morning. She would walk all perimeters in a very methodical and focused manner each morning. She needed to assess, to take stock, to make sure all was well for all of us. Since she's been gone, the little ones, have ever so gradually started to take over some of Gil's tasks—but let's not kid ourselves. Though Gilda did teach the Havanese to be good little Dachshunds, there will never be a worker like Gilda. Oh, another thing that they are starting to do that was Gilda's job is to dry people off when they are wet from the pool. Gilda would march around the perimeter of the pool and if anyone would come up to her, she would feel it was her responsibility to dry off their arms, hands, face, etc. Neatness, order, work—all were extremely high values for Gilda.

Gilda was also in charge of most any home projects that occurred. She, like myself, did not love home projects. But I know she felt that if she kept very close inspection on everything that was being done, and kept order to the chaos, it would all turn out well. She was right! She was very good and adaptable with any home projects. Some she got used to—like putting up and taking down the Christmas decorations. She understood that when all the bins came out this meant that soon there would be all sorts of seasonal items in our home—like trees! But that after a season, and probably many visitors, it would all go back to "normal." Gilda—like all my dogs—understood the seasons of life. I think they really get the passage from scripture that says, "there is a time for all things: a time to laugh, a time to cry, a time for rest, a time for work, and so on." One spring we put in a new deck. This was a big project and meant quite a new routine for the dogs for a short time. They adapted as usual, but Gilda, once again, amazed all of us with her workmanship! At one point in the process there were only joist boards across the whole deck area. It looked like a maze. Gilda, of course, had to go under the deck to inspect, and then she had to keep popping her head up through the joists to show us where she was. It was so funny; all our friends who were working were once again in total laughter at Gilda.

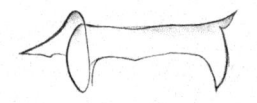

CHAPTER 15
Passionate Kisses

Let's talk about kisses. Dog kisses are very distinct, and different kisses say different things. Let me start by reminding you that I am a fanatic when it comes to cleanliness and neatness, so, the irony here lies in the fact that for a reason that makes no sense whatsoever, I find dog kisses to be a very spiritual thing—so much so that I find different meanings in them. And yet, I am not quite as free with my human affections. Interesting. Anyway, back to the pooches! So, Maggie and Karly gave very gentle and only-if-you-want-it pecks. They were a little hesitant about it, but wanted to give you this sign of affection, but they would never impose it upon you if you were "not in the mood"—so very Karly-ish! Gilda and Eleanor gave the type of kisses that are given because they think you need them!

Gilda used to literally smash her face upon your face and kiss you like it was her job. She was quite affectionate, quite expressive, and quite passionate. I took this to mean, "You are mine and I gotcha—always." Oh, she loved getting the affection back at times when she needed it, but she did not always need it. Interesting, though, was if I wanted to give Gil kisses and she wasn't needing them, she would let me anyway. How sweet is that? And then there is Eleanor, the baby, whom has yet to be "formally introduced," but she kisses like Gil did. Eli does many things like Gil, because for the first year of her life she followed and idolized every move that Gilda made and she indeed has taken on some of Gil's characteristics. Very amazing! Eli does like a good "open mouth" kiss at times—sorry, had to be honest! The thing that I find amazing about dogs and their giving of affection is that they are so very humble and unobtrusive about it. They will give you all they have, but not if you are not ready for it. God waits for us to be ready all the time—to receive his love and care. Perhaps our dogs are showing us this as well.

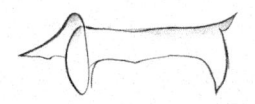

CHAPTER 16
Forgive and Forget

I think one of the most powerful things I've felt from my dogs is patience and forgiveness, sometimes shown through the abovementioned kisses, other times just shown through the way they look at you, or give you their belly. Dogs are the most patient and forgiving creatures I know. I can't say that I've ever done anything that would merit huge forgiveness from them, thankfully, but certainly on a day-to-day basis I'm far less than perfect—and they forgive. I know through the years, even when I was having a human moment relating to anything where I messed up, if I sat with this, I could always find Gilda coming up alongside of me and seeming to ponder things with me. I would feel from her some consolation. She seemed to be communicating to me that it was ok; we are all bound to make a mistake or two, and I was still good and lovable. She would assure me with those eyes or kisses that she loved me unconditionally. There have been times, of course, when I've lost my patience with them—Gil or the others—and yelled too loud or gotten frustrated. Again, though, they would use their best judgment to either stop the behavior; they would then come back to mend the relationship. Wow—have I learned much from this. I know that I sometimes, with other relationships, hold onto anger or hurt too long—not real long, and this I have my dear mom to be grateful for. She has always taught and lived to be kind and forgiving and nonjudgmental—always. So between my amazing mom, and these amazing dogs in my life, hopefully any judgmental part of me doesn't stand a chance. Because, really, why would we hold onto things? And, is it really our place to judge someone else? Doesn't love and forgiveness and understanding and compassion feel so very much better and go to those higher places?

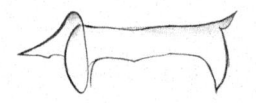

CHAPTER 17
And Then There Were Three!

It is interesting now, in retrospect, to realize how much Gilda was preparing Karly, during her two years with her, to eventually be the leader. But Karly would be a much different kind of leader than Gilda. Some beings are born to be leaders—like Gilda—some are taught and step up—like Karly. Oh, and then there is Eleanor . . . the baby!

Eleanor came along one year after Gilda and Karly became sisters. We knew, because in some very mysterious and amazing ways, Gilda was telling us that she might not be with us for very much longer in the big scheme of things. So, we found Eleanor to join our family. Eleanor picked us, just like Karly did. She is a Havanese and a blood sister of Karly, eleven months younger. Like Karls, when we went to the pet store to meet her, she jumped into my arms and began to kiss me on the mouth. A bit forward, yes, but did she win me over within five kisses . . . maybe four, yes, of course! So, Eleanor came home that night to Gilda, Karly, and us. We took about two weeks and seven names to come up with Eleanor. We decided on Eleanor because she showed us early on that she has guts, personality plus, is very tenacious, yet can be a little shy all at once (especially with new people and dogs). She has good boundaries. But her tenacity and spunk shone through quite quickly and we liked Eleanor after Eleanor Roosevelt—a person whom Nancy and I both truly admire. So, in came Eli! I call Karly our Hippie and Eleanor our Beatnik! She's a toughie, kind of a tomboy, but a baby as well. I can relate to all this. She wants to act big, to be part of the older siblings, to imitate what they do, to learn things very quickly—but then she turns around and is such a baby as well. Again, being the youngest sibling of seven myself, I can totally relate to Eli. Gilda, again, had another Havanese to train to be a good dachshund. And between Karly and Eli, Eli has definitely picked up more of Gilda's traits than Karly did. She would follow Gilda's every move. And, she tried like heck for several months to show Gil how much fun she could be. Gilda, though as kind and good as the day is long, took a little bit of patience for a while with Eleanor. And here's where the circle continues, because lo and behold, Karly began to be the mediator with Eleanor and Gilda. When Gilda would get impatient, Karly would literally set a pick between the two of them. Or, she would just get near to Gilda and distract her from her impatience. Or, she would entertain the baby so that she'd stop bugging Gilda. It was truly amazing and brilliant of Karly, and it worked! Karly began to show that there are many kinds of leaders in life. She, is a gentle leader—a mediator, a peacemaker. Like I said, she's our little Ghandi. And, Gilda, interestingly, allowed Karls to start to take some responsibilities. It's as if she really knew that she had to start empowering Karly to take over some things for her, because she would not be with us forever. The next year with the three of them together would be a wonderful year for us all—and very hard in some ways as well—as Gilda prepared to leave us. Life is so very full of circles. It is full of deep love and deep pain, and God gave us these three in that last year to experience it all together.

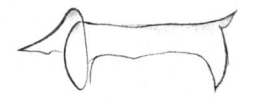

CHAPTER 18
Rock It!

We had such great times during that year. Our third summer in this home, the gardens were a flourishing, the pool was wonderfully welcoming to all our family and friends, and these three little ones became the life of the party very often. They loved pool party days, which was basically every day off that the weather was good. They loved to work outside with us in the morning—pool prepping, staging things, gardening, fixing good-smelling foods and drinks in the kitchen—and ultimately they knew that this meant that some of their favorite people would be arriving soon to play. Somehow, Gil, Karl, and Eli knew this was all so fortunate and good; they reveled in it with us. And, they loved the friends and family who all loved them so much. It was/is a happy place, where we celebrate the love that surrounds us by creating a beautiful atmosphere to do so. Oh, and the music—everyone loves the music—not the least of which is the girls. On a couple occasions per summer we have big bashes which include karaoke! We all especially get excited for this—well, let's be honest—Gilda and I got excited for this. Gilda knew karaoke for years. We'd always loved to entertain, and so throwing big fun parties was part of Gilda's life experience, and she dug it. She worked hard with me for all of it. And, unlike her baby sisters now, Gilda's stamina would prevail during any big bash. Gilda was first one up with us in the morning preparing things, and the last one standing at night cleaning up. For real, she was "on it"—all of it. She also loved when I sang Karaoke—or at least she understood that I loved to sing karaoke and so she took great delight and pride in my singing. She would often meander her way over to the microphone area where I was singing and come up into my arms while I performed. Gilda loved her music and dance—she felt the awesomeness of music and dance, like so many of us understand. It was soothing, moving, and fun for her—all at once. Music is the language of the soul and Gil sure did get this one. Side note—Gilda's appreciation of my karaoke singing was out of pure love; I'm not that good, really. I'm fair, but my Gilda made me feel like a star! And, don't we all want to give this gift to those we love?

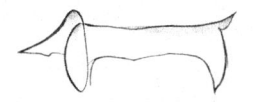

CHAPTER 19
Spring is in the Air!

And then started Eleanor's first spring in life! Can you imagine the delight of a puppy when she discovers spring—oh my! The sounds, the sights, the scents, the things to roll in! I think that every human being—especially when reaching that "midlife" time of our journey—should at least observe, if not have, a puppy in the spring, just to remind us. Ahhhh—to remind us of what a powerfully spectacular thing God's nature really is.

Eleanor is tough and all shy, all at once, as I said. If she really knows you are "one of hers," she will approach you with some loving biting and then open-mouth kissing. If she is not sure that you belong in her world, she will hightail it out of the area and not return 'til you are gone. This is kinda what Eleanor is like with most things—all or nothing. She plays like mad and then crashes out with intent. When she lays down, she slams her eyes shut as if to say, "Ok, I'm going to sleep NOW." When she wants a little affection or a little forgiveness (she sometimes might just do a puppy-like thing), she slams over on her back to give you the belly, or she puts her head down right in your lap so you scratch her head and ears. She is also kind of a scrapper—she's the Baby. She takes what she can get but doesn't demand much at all. Eleanor is also teaching me something about diligence, and again, like so many dogs, doing the right thing. Even as a young puppy, she surely wants to please. She tries to go along with the program and seems to understand very keenly what the "program" is—whether set by her two older sisters, or by us. So, if it's time to rest, she will rest. If it is time to play, she will play. If it is time to snuggle, she will snuggle. Again, she does it all with strong intent—always. When she was still sleeping in her crate, she would be playing around 'til the last minute and then we'd tell her it was time for sleep, put her in her crate, and slam—she'd lay down and go to sleep. She is such a good girl, really. So many of our dogs show us time and time again to live life, on life's terms. We also like to refer to Eleanor at times as a "hot mess"! She does get herself kinda jazzed up sometimes with her roughhousing type of spirit. She, Karly, and sometimes Gilly, would literally tear-ass around our yard, poolside, and deck for what was one of the greatest shows on earth. Eleanor, of course, is the daredevil in this show. She will tear around the pool, cutting corners as if there is no water near her. She and the others are all quite amazing about the pool too.

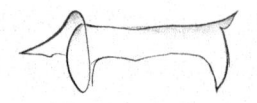

CHAPTER 20
Splish-Splash

Gilda has always known and understood water. She swam in it once or twice—didn't love it, didn't hate it, loved the activity of it. Kinda like her momma—me! One time, when Gilly was a pup, we were up at the lake house with my sister and brother-in-law. We took the dogs out on the boat: Gilda, Maggie, and Chester, who was also Gilda's age. Chester was already familiar with the boat, the lake, and the routine. He was so pleased and happy to have his two friends and cousins along to show the fun to. So, we parked at this "tailgating" type area, where people get out of their boats, play, swim, picnic—all in the water. It's a gas. So, we decide to let the dogs swim, as many people do. For what seemed like an endless amount of delightful time, the three of them took turns jumping off the boat and into mine and Dick's arms.

My sister, Rose Ann, stayed on the boat and announced: "Here comes Chester on the right," "Here comes Gilda on the left," "Here comes Maggie on the right"! It was a riot; everyone around was watching the show. Dick and I were getting our workout, and the dogs were having the time of their life—jumping, being caught, swimming back. Wow, what a memory. We all had a very tired and relaxing boat ride back on the lake that day.

So, Gil would guard and clean people off in the pool, but she didn't love swimming in it the couple times we tried. She was happy to patrol. Karly wants no part of the pool except for the parties that it generates. When Gil would get too close in patrol mode, Karly stayed back and turned in circles; she still does this when Eleanor pulls her stunts. Eleanor, on the other hand, believes that this big pool—like most of life to her—is her playground. Early on, during her first winter and spring, she began to run across the pool cover. We were all a bit shocked and then found it all quite hilarious. She bounces across it like it's her own private, huge trampoline. She likes to show us all that life can be such a discovery and so much fun if you look for the fun. She also goes out onto the diving board and just looks around. She has never been in the pool, and we are very grateful that all of our girls learned their boundaries with the pool and how to stay safe. Again, brilliant beyond belief!

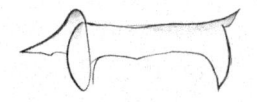

CHAPTER 21
The Pack

Gil, Karls, and Eli became quite the pack. They developed their own rhythm to life together. They learned the ways and needs of one another. There was really very, very little disagreeing among them—hardly ever. They loved to wrestle and play and even learned the order of how to do this together all three. Eli would play very wild and crazy with Karly, because Karly could take it and tolerate it. But when Eli would play with Gilda she toned it down and allowed Gilda to determine the level of play. We often found ourselves just simply watching the three of them interact because I think we knew that they had so very much to show us. Karl and Eli would definitely take Gil's lead on most things. Sometimes, I'm not sure if they even knew why they were barking or where they were going, but they trusted Gilda implicitly—as they should have—to lead them to good works . . . and play. They also became quite good at accommodating each other in the resting mode. For a while, we had Eli crated for sleeping at night and for a "while" she went along with it. We'd get Gilly and Karly in their bed in our room and then Eli would know it was time for her to sleep in her crate. After about six months Eleanor started to desire to sleep with her sisters. So, out we went to get a nice day bed that would accommodate three sleeping dogs. And, lo and behold, within about two to three days all three dogs had learned happily that this was their bed for three. They adjusted positions for a while, but then all got used to their spots. And, I know they found great comfort again in the consistency and dependability of this being their bed, right next to ours, where they all slept together. Oh and we finally got a routine where they can come on the "big bed" with us in the early morning for a while, or during weekend naps. So they basically even adapted to and learned this—that they go to sleep in their bed and then get the treat to come in the big bed for mornings and rests. Again, what incredible learning and discipline and accommodating that they all three displayed.

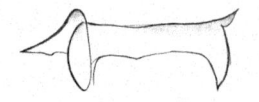

CHAPTER 22
Saying Good-Bye for Now

This last year of our time here on earth with Gilda—and with all three of them together—brought us all five so much utter joy and then some utter pain. One thing that happened in our life during the early part of that year was that Nancy's elderly mom declined in her health and then passed away. This was, of course, an extremely difficult time for Nancy and all of us around her. The three girls—Gil, Karl, and even baby Eli—knew that there was sadness going on and they knew that Nancy was in pain. It was often the case that you would find any one, or all three of them, cuddling up to her on the couch, giving her comfort and closeness. Or, they would lick her hands and kiss her face; they knew. They knew it was time for us to care for her and her grief. Selfless love is what all three gave to Nancy during that most difficult time.

And, while this was happening, Gilda began to develop some serious health issues herself. Gilda was twelve years old in the last year of her life and developed a condition called Chronic Rhinitis. Gilda would show us all what it takes to say good-bye to this part of your life while taking care of those she loved, remaining dignified, strong, patient, and loving, and never giving up on living to her fullest to the end. Wow, if I could exemplify these virtues when the end of this life comes for me, I would feel I had done so well at transitioning.

Gilda's condition started to seriously manifest itself in early winter of that year. To sum it up, we went through a year with her, trying every medical solution possible, including some procedures, trying to keep things in our environment better for her condition, trying to just let it naturally take its course, and everything in between. Rhinitis is a chronic inflammation and disease of the nasal passages. It cannot be cured, only dealt with. To the best of our understanding, Gilda lived with what would feel like a constant, major sinus infection, including the coughing, sneezing, discharge, and pain. My question became, very quickly, how long would I allow Gil to be in this pain and discomfort, or how long until she would let me know that we needed to say good-bye to her. She gave us another eleven months, and, she gave all she had. This presented me with so much to learn about life. End of life issues with any being we love will present this. As all of us know with dogs that the very perplexing issue is that ultimately we choose when it is time. Please do not take this the wrong way, but I will say that I have wished upon more than one occasion that we didn't have to make that choice, and then at other times that we were able to make that choice with everyone. But, we do not . . . just with our pets. These precious, higher beings, who understand and exemplify God's love so brilliantly—God then lets us decide. It is both a privilege and a most difficult thing. I have always said, that I would not let any dog of mine suffer unnecessarily. They bring such amazing love to this world, and we have this responsibility to decide for them, so I will decide before their life becomes anything but pleasant. It's the very least I can do, really. This is not meant to be a sad book, but it is important to be aware of all that dogs teach us, even in their end of life time. It is my intention here to heighten all of our awarenesses to higher places, to honor our dogs who have given us this, and to ultimately praise God for giving us them. So, no, this is not about Gilda's death—it is about how she and all our loved dogs lived their lives.

Gilda struggled through many ups and downs that year. Some of the things she enjoyed the most started to be a struggle for her, though she would never give up or stop doing them. Two examples of this are taking walks and wrestling around with her sisters. Both were two of Gil's happiest times—especially when with any of her sisters or her pack. But this last year, almost every day, Gil would have a breathing issue along the way on each and every walk. Oh, she would stick it out and she would still be the leader and she would still want to go further than all three of the rest of us, but it was hard on her. She would never let on to me, though, that it was hard. She wanted to please and care for me every step of her life. It was the same with the wrestling with Karl and Eli. She wanted to show them that she loved them—she loved the puppiness and life within them—but she would often go into a coughing or sneezing attack while playing, for which the babies would simply back away and let her recover and then they would all resume. Often Gil would have messy discharge, many times a day throughout this year, and she even tried to take care of this. We made sure we had proper wipes around at all times to quickly clean her up and tell her she was doing a good job dealing with her breathing/nasal disease and we all tried so very much to preserve her dignity. Gilda had a lot of dignity—she liked to do the right things, act the right way, and not make a mess of anything, anytime. She, like me, felt it an honor to be among such love and life and we wanted to always "earn our keep." Gilda used to come in from the yard and spend several minutes grooming herself from her playtime. You never, ever had to worry about Gil being a mess—she wouldn't have it. Funny thing is, this is one of the many characteristics that Eleanor has picked up from Gilda. She now comes in from the yard and spends several minutes grooming herself. Oh my!

It is also quite amazing to us that both Karly and Eleanor have manifested so many qualities and characteristics of Molly and Gilda. Again, the circle of life, the hope of God is beyond our wildest imaginings. So, interestingly, Karly never met Molly. Karls came to us one week after we said good-bye to Molly. But almost immediately we started to be amazed at some of the characteristics of Karly that were Molly's. Now, one might think, "Well, dogs do a lot of similar things," and yes, they do. Just like people—we all scratch when we itch, we sneeze, we walk, talk—but I'm telling you, this was not about common characteristics. For example, Molly liked to walk in straight lines; she was not real agile or super athletic, so she always chose a cautious, sure-thing path. Karls does the same thing. We brought her home and she started moving like Molly.

She also had identical eyes as Molly—almost freakily so. She also eats like Molly, takes bites like Molly, played with Gilda just like Molly did, and so on. We were moved beyond words, really, as Karly began to show us that Molly's spirit had somehow brought her to us and was now here to stay through Karls. Then there is Ms. Eleanor, who literally hung on Gilda's every move and breath. I believe that she and Gil had a special bond for Gilda was preparing her to carry on some of her traditions and characteristics for our home and family. For example, Eleanor has begun moving pinecones and burrowing everywhere! (Havanese just don't burrow—dachshunds do!) She grooms herself and barks like Gil at the same things Gilda did, and so on. We all are given great comfort in the loss of Molly and Gilda to have their characteristics live on in Karly and Eli. We are all so very connected, and the passing on of life strings is forever. Hope is a great gift from God.

Side note on the burrowing, and actually, there is no lesson here, it's just plain old cute! So, Eleanor, as mentioned, has begun burrowing. Now, mind you, if you understand the breed of Havanese, they really do not burrow. Karls, for example likes to lie down on flat, cool surfaces. She does not like to be covered, or buried, or make this kind of "nest" for herself. Eli, however, has followed Gilda's every move to the tee and so she believes that burrowing is the right thing to do when she goes to get settled in. However, the funny part of this is that she's, well, not so good at it. Now, mind you, it's a tough act to follow for sure—Gil was an expert burrower. It was an art. Eli, however, ends up usually displacing the blanket or burrowing area onto the floor and her hair will be standing straight up in the air from static. She works so very hard to create the space, it takes several minutes, and then she comes up a mess with no blanket. We laugh; Karls just shakes her head at the baby, and we know that some day El will grow up to be a good burrower, the way her sister Gilda was!

Speaking of hope, I have come to understand that having puppies is a sure thing kind of way to never get too sad. Truly. There is something amazing and brilliant about the wonder and love of a puppy. They remind us that every day is indeed a new beginning. They remind us that there is wonder in everyday ordinary life. They remind us to play. They remind us to laugh. They remind us to cuddle and love. They remind us that, yes, we all will get a little mischievous once in a while or do something wrong, but we must forgive and love on—every time. Perhaps if we all just rolled on our backs and looked super cute we'd all get a lot more forgiveness when we make a mistake. There are times when my mood might be less than positive, and every time, if I put my hands on Karly or Eli's bellies, rub their heads, or scratch behind their ears, the love that this generates keeps me out of the blues. So, lesson given to us—love truly conquers all and there is really no reason for a bad day if we have this hope and believe.

So, as the year progressed we began to listen to what Gilda was telling us, preparing us for, and showing us. It was a rough year indeed, but one filled with so very many lessons and awakenings. All dogs prepare themselves and their humans for their good-bye. We've all seen and heard how they start to move away from the pack a bit more, spend more time alone, preparing us all for the earthly separation that ultimately has to take place. Gilda was quite amazing in this. She not only started to prepare us, she also took care of us when she saw we were sad. Many a time, I'd be sitting, pondering what was to come, and Gil would just come up on my lap and start licking me—hands, legs, etc. It was as if she was trying to comfort and fix me—all the time. She shared her love with all of us, too. She would give extra comfort to Nancy, who was also grieving her mom; she would take care of the puppies all the time. She just never stopped giving. I don't know if I can ever be as giving as Gilda was, but I know that another reason God gave her to me was to show me how to be so. So that I can strive, always, to live in these higher places that Gilda lived in every day—and, again, with no complaints. She did not run from her pain; she did not have the choice to mask or medicate it. She trusted me to care for what she needed and she stayed loving and positive most always through it all. You know, I just can't be more in awe than this.

When it came time to say good-bye, we prepared ourselves as best as possible. Gilda got to see all the people she knew and loved and they her. We kept things positive but true—that was Gilda, true. The last day, I tried to think what last thing I could give her to show her how much I loved her. Really, there weren't "things" or "food" that could express this, but I tried. So, Nanc brought home a cinnamon coffee cake—one of Gilda's favorite people foods. I spent the last couple hours with her doing her favorite earthly things. We went for a great walk—all of us, of course. We came home and the little ones went to our friend's next door for a couple hours. It was so helpful and kind of them to care for Karl and Eli during this time. So then Gil and I shared some cinnamon coffee cake, alone! We then went for a ride in the car, with all the windows down, and listened to the song Ben by MJ—I love this song and it reminds me of my love for Gil. And that was it. I held her and we said good-bye. Then the girls came home so they could understand she was gone; she was gone from this earthly life. I understand fully that to love deeply means to lose deeply. It's ok; it's all part of the circle of life. But I will honestly say that this has been the greatest loss of my life—one like no other. And yet, I know it was right and correct, as Gilda would have it. And, most importantly, I know Gilda is with God, in Heaven, in a joyful, painless, love-filled place that we will all get to some day. So what is more amazing is how even after Gilda left us, she—and God—have taught me and given me so much it is hard to put into words. It is as if, when they leave us, our dogs, they can work with God's goodness even more now to love and help the world. The love of God that comes through in our animals is beyond words. When Gilda was first gone, I literally was lost—so lost. I felt that she defined me and helped make me who I was, and I wondered how would I know what defined me now. And, low and behold, during my grieving process, and through prayer and such sadness, I have found that this experience is defining and redefining me even more. So, what is amazing is that I believe that Gilda's showing me how to live in higher places is taking place even more now that she is in Heaven with God. God's wisdom and goodness are so huge.

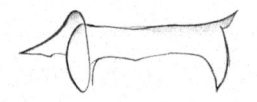

CHAPTER 23
Ch-Ch-Ch-Changes

It was a very sad and hard time in our home for a while after Gilda left. All of us were quite lost and seeming to need more naps and quiet time, which we had. Karly did a lot of howling. As I said, I wished I could howl; I would have. It ached for all of us. And, we were not sure just who was in charge anymore. We could laugh and joke about this a bit, but the reality is that Gilda was such an amazing presence in our world and our lives it was hard to imagine who would be her presence. Nancy was explaining this to my niece, Dana, one night, and Dana, in her amazing wisdom and kindness, said to Nancy, "Well, perhaps you or my Auntie Annette might consider being in charge"! We got the biggest kick out of this, and also admitted to Dana that we didn't know if we could. We would all walk around asking the question, "What would Gilda do?". As months have gone on, I have come to understand that Gilda truly was a guiding force in my life. I am completely convinced that God gives us exactly what we need, when we need it, if we are open to this. For those of us who have been "given" dogs, God, again, knew exactly what we needed and when, and God sends these precious little beings to show us the way! I now know that Gilda was my guiding force for the past twelve years of my life, and in some ways, she saved my life, over and over and over again. I also know now, in her absence from my day to day life, that she now sits next to—or on—God's lap and assists God in guiding me to even higher places now.

I am a person who, like so many, needs purpose, structure, and order—as much as we have control over these things! When Gilda came to me, she began to define me in a new way. I had never given birth to a child and she gave me a purpose and structure to life that I would not have otherwise found, and, she knew this—believe me, she knew this every day of our life together. And, God knew that I needed these things. God puts things—people, events, animals—in our paths just when we need them; it is truly amazing. And, as Gilda was preparing to leave this earthly life, she was also preparing me to learn from my life with her what

I needed and how start to apply it, how to live it. It astounds me how this little being is teaching me some of the strongest life lessons—ones that are literally saving me—even after she is gone from here. The adjustment has been difficult, to say the least, but I am positive every day that there is a purpose to all the transitioning and grief as well.

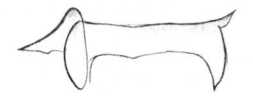

CHAPTER 24
Adjusting

Karly and Eleanor are doing their share of transitioning, too. They were, at first, completely lost. We began to resume our walks immediately, but this would be the first time in their lives where Gilda was not leading them. We hoped that Karls would step up, and she eventually did, but it took her a bit of grieving time as well. And we all allowed it of one another, as did our friends and family. Again, from Ecclesiastes we learn that there is a time for all things under the sun—a time for joy, a time for sadness, a time to laugh, a time to cry. Karly and Eleanor seemed to show us how to move with this seasonal view, for they both did their share of grieving, but then little by little they stepped out of that state and into the development of a new pack—one with just the two of them and us. And, they have begun to come into their own as Havanese rather than little dachshunds. Oh, they don't have to necessarily love it all the time, and I know they still miss Gilda, but they, like Gilda, do the right thing. They live life, on life's terms. Eleanor began to be more independent and obviously not dependent on Gilly's every lead, and Karly began to show a brave side to herself that we never knew! Keep in mind, Eli moves and does everything with deliberation and strong intent, while Karly does everything gently and a bit hesitantly. But, they both kind of stepped toward each other after Gilda was gone. Eli isn't so reckless and crazy anymore, and even shows a cautious and disciplined side once in a while. Karly musters up all she has and gets brave to be near or take care of her adventuresome little sis. It is precious and amazing to watch how they have gradually and naturally stepped up during and as a result of this great time of loss for us all.

We have actually discovered what I would call an assertiveness to Eleanor. This is also a great lesson to learn from. Eli actually has great boundaries. She is willing and desiring to explore and try new things—but she knows her limits. And, she knows how to take space away from a situation if she needs some space. She knows how to breath. For such a young girl, this is pretty impressive. I think she learned a little bit how to be "older" than her age, having grown up her first year with Gilda as her leader and Karly as her big sister. She knows how to set limits for herself. She knows that "no" means "no" and "yes" means "yes." Though she wants to please us, she still knows her boundaries and is not afraid to assert them. I actually teach this principle to children about safety—to know their boundaries and learn to be assertive. I feel that dear Eleanor is here to show us all that some healthy boundaries are actually more loving and honest than anything else.

So, we've all been transitioning for the past several months—together and individually, all of us. And it is interesting how much each of us knows what each other is going through. Sometimes I know that Karly and Eleanor allow me that extra time to rest, or be sad, or to feverishly work in the yard, or many of the things I do to care for my grief for Gilda. Instincts of dogs are amazing. Karly and Eli have grown up a lot from the loss of Gil, and on another level, they have come into their own as puppies. We all know that this is exactly what Gilda would want for us. We had an exceptionally warm month of March this year, so we were outside a lot—much earlier than we would have normally been. It was clear that this was difficult and new for all of us, to be out in our yard, the place that held so many memories of Gil's presence, without her being physically with us here. One day, as has happened countless times, I was made incredibly aware of Gilda's and God's blessing on us all, every day. We were doing some spring cleaning. It was a beautiful day—almost eighty degrees, there was a slight breeze, Karls and Eli were having a blast running around the yard, and Nanc and I were working and enjoying the day. Upon many occasions on that almost first day outside without Gil I felt her presence so very strongly. It was bittersweet, of course, because I am so very human and I miss her so very much. But I allowed the message to come, as it has constantly since Gil left us, that "it is all as it should be." The gentle breeze actually was caressing my mind and soul and telling me it was time to transition, time to let Gilly be in a new place with the best love in the world—God's love. My pain was not in vain—it was all a gift for having loved and learned so much from Gilda and all her kin. I was and am so incredibly fortunate to have learned all this about God. So let it turn, Annette; let the breeze blow through. Let the puppies be who they are now, and so on. It was a March day that I will never forget—mostly because I know that God was speaking to me with Gilda by God's side. Oh, I miss my Gilly in my gardens; she was a part of my love for gardening that runs deep. It was Gilly and my gardens, hand in hand. We put a beautiful dachshund angel in our garden, next to the St. Francis; these things and reminders of this kind of love all belong together. It is as it should be, in a profound sort of way. But, God's love is beyond profound, really.

Karly and Eli have begun to share in new ways, and actually, watching a dog share and wait for their turn is something I learn from every day. But Karls, as mentioned earlier, will sometimes wait to eat her treats that are given to her. It's like she kinda likes to relish the idea of it for a while, play with it, guard it, simply treasure it. In the past, Eleanor would start to meander around her and her treat and there would often be a tad bit of low growling by Karl to tell Eli that this was hers and to back off. Low and behold, Eleanor has learned to respect this. Now, Karly can leave a treat of hers in a spot for as long as she chooses; Eleanor will stroll around it to inspect, but she never, ever goes after it anymore, and Karl does not need to remind her anymore that it is her treasure she is saving. Ahhhhh—they are just such good beings.

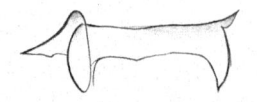

CHAPTER 25
More Razz

Have you ever witnessed a good game of "razz" in session? Most of us have, I'm sure, if you're reading this book and thus, love dogs. If you get two or more dogs together and they become comfortable with each other, they begin and love to play razz. I love this game and often wish I could play it with others, too. I do actually play it with my dogs, which is one of the times that I wonder if I'm not part dog . . . hmmm. In any case, razz is the game where two or more dogs begin razzing each other up. There is soft biting of each other's ears, tails, and paws involved. There is also much diving and dashing and running faster than you can imagine this little being can run, and more dive-bombing into each other and open-mouthed playing, etc. Oh, and then there are the sounds: monster-like growling, humming, moaning, panting, and the like. Gilda, Karly, and Eli played razz like no others, though as mentioned earlier, when Gilda joined the game it was catered to her pace, which is amazing and accommodating of Karls and Eli to know. Now, with just Karly and Eli, the game is ramped up quite a few notches and goes on and on forever. What I love about this game the most is watching the sheer joy and play that they are feeling for each other and for life. They play like there is no other moment, and most interesting is that there is not the goal of having a winner or a loser. Oh no, the game is played just merely for the sake of the game. We as humans often feel the sense of competition in games or even in life. Dogs don't play this way. They play hard because it is fun and life is joyful for them at that moment. I wish and hope that I am learning to enjoy the moments like this. I have a long way to go but am again thankful for my dogs teaching me this holy lesson.

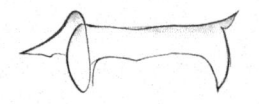

CHAPTER 26
Ordinary Days

On the other end of this spectrum, my dogs have shown me so much about the beauty of stillness and quiet. There is nothing more holy to me than to feel or watch the belly going up and down on one of my sleeping dogs. They love to rest. But as mentioned earlier, they love to work and play hard, too. But they sure do know how to rest, and how to bask in the goodness of a good rest. All of my dogs have always presented to me a total relaxation and calm when they are in a quiet place. Gilda, as I've mentioned previously, used to love to bask in a sunbeam, or listen to some peaceful John Denver music. Karls loves the soft breeze and quiet. Eli, too, seems to love when things quieten down in her world—she, of course, hits the couch or whatever it is she chooses to lay on hard and fast and is out. This is El—deliberate, most often. They have also all shown me how much they love music and even my singing to them. Oh, truly, I'm not the best singer in the world, but I used to hold Gil and sing her songs and she would just sit there and relax as I sang to her. They all know the total holiness of God's gift of stillness. They have given me a sense of steadiness, not just in their resting, but in their consistency with life. They are steady and dependable in all that they do. In scripture we are told, "Be still and know I am your God." Yes, our dogs know this; please keep showing me this way.

Speaking of God and stillness—Easter morning this past year was an instance when I was given such clarity and calm, and I am sure it was given to me by God having Gilda being right by his side. It was kind of like that beautiful day in March that I spoke of earlier. It was a perfect day—beautiful temperature, bright sunshine, moderate breeze, everything around us was blooming with vibrancy. It was quiet; it was peaceful. The only thing missing was my Gilda, but as has happened on so many occasions since she left us, she showed me that day that she was good, full of love in Heaven, and that everything was as it was supposed to be. You see, I'm not one to believe that life is meant to be easy. Oh, I'm not all about suffering either, mind you, but like my dogs, I think I've just always known that life here on earth is a journey, one that we are meant to learn much about how to be more spiritual people, until we meet with God and all the celestial beings in Heaven. I'm ok with this. But as a result, we will have some pain and sorrow on this level. But what I heard and felt deeply that morning was that only through the growing pains of this part of our journey do we get to the resurrection of Easter, the rapture of Heaven with the One who is ALL LOVE—our God. So I felt a sense of things as they should be that morning. The little ones and I had a wonderful walk, as we often do. But that day, it seemed that we all came to "our stride" again a bit—even without the presence of Gil. It was a gift. It amazes me, that even after our dogs are gone, they still continue to teach and show us things about how to live in higher places while they sit in the embrace and guidance of God.

I have felt this help from Gilda and Molly very strongly after they both left us. With Molly, as I previously mentioned, I felt she led us to Karly and embodied Karly with some of her gentle spirit. I kept hearing things in my heart that were Molly-like messages, like how to breath better, how to trust that you will get what you need in life, and how to be gentle and appreciative—always. Since Gilda has gone to Heaven, it is quite amazing how much she has helped me. I have gained so much insight and clarity into being a better person and also felt her strength literally carrying me through. Oh, I don't just mean carrying me through the grief of missing her; I mean carrying me through normal day-to-day life. I often call upon the strength that Gilda lived with when I have to do something unpleasant. I think about how Gilda lived every day, just doing the right thing, and I truly believe that this, she, God, is making me a better person. It has also been a time when my faith has grown stronger, because I feel Gil's presence so strongly that I know for sure she is with God. Many of us have grieved the loss of loved ones in our lives. I know I have. Somehow, I feel that dogs—again, being such spiritual beings—have a way of strengthening our faith and strengthening our goodness, even after they are gone from us physically. Not long ago, I was having a day when I was missing Gil particularly strongly. I said to myself, "I wish I could dream about Gilda today." That evening, I had an amazingly peaceful dream about Gil. She simply came to me; I held her, I squeezed her, I kissed her. She gave me the same in return and then the dream was over. Truly astounding, but yet, when I think about the awesomeness of God, and how Gil is now working with God, it shouldn't be astounding at all. But, I'm very human, very flawed, and need these spiritual lessons over and over and over.

Here is one more: so this spring here in Chicago was an unusual one, weather-wise. It was a quite mild winter, and the month of March was like early May—warm temps, blooming nature, gentle winds. It was very different. April, then, became more "March-like," and so on. In any case, Mother Nature has been, of course, adapting to all of this, and one of the many interesting phenomenons is that there is a tremendous amount of butterflies! I don't mean just a lot—I mean like flocks of them, everywhere! Wow—what a beautiful thing, because really, who doesn't get her spirit lifted and see true signs of resurrection and new life from butterflies. I believe that Gilda is wanting me to see the enormous truth about resurrection and new life through these butterflies. Oh, I'm not saying Gilda made it happen . . . though I wonder . . . but I know the message. I hear it, I see it, and I've always needed strong messages, strong flavors, etc. So no, there aren't just a few butterflies this spring—there are literally flocks of them! Thank you, God—I get it.

There are so many lessons to learn each day of our lives, if and when we are awake to them. People, events, nature, and our animals are all gifts and vehicles of God's to teach us how to live life in higher places. That is why we are here. We are here in human form to learn how to be more spiritual; that is the purpose. And to me, our dogs in particular have been the most powerful teacher of this. Again, no disrespect to the many, many God-moments I have shared with the human relationships I am privileged to be in as well. My mom is an example of this. She is a very humble and gentle person. There are a couple of things she has said and examples she has given us that guide my life every day. She has always suggested to me that moderation will be a great balancing guide for me. She is right. She has always shown me acceptance and nonjudgementalness. She is so right on with this. And, she has always practiced kindness wherever she has gone. Seemingly, my mom and Gilda are probably two of the strongest beings who have helped and taught me how to strive for higher places. I'm fifty years old. I'm quite sure, and hopeful, that I have many more years to learn, and I'm just as sure that the lessons that my dogs have taught me will keep on revealing themselves to me. I can only hope.

So folks, enjoy the gift of our dogs, and pay attention: I believe that God is teaching us all sorts of wonderful life lessons through them. God wants us to live in higher places, and they seem to get that. They also get that simple sniffing in the scents of each new moment helps us to be present in the moment and love what is there.

Peace. Namaste!